OUTRAGEOUS CLIP ART

for Youth Ministry

Illustrations by Rand Kruback

Group Books

Loveland, Colorado

Dedication

This book is dedicated to Uncle Josh and all
the people who like to draw laughs but can't.

Outrageous Clip Art for Youth Ministry

Copyright © 1988 by Rand Kruback

Fourth Printing, 1991

Credits

Cover design by Judy Atwood

ISBN 0931-529-39-5

Printed in the United States of America

Contents

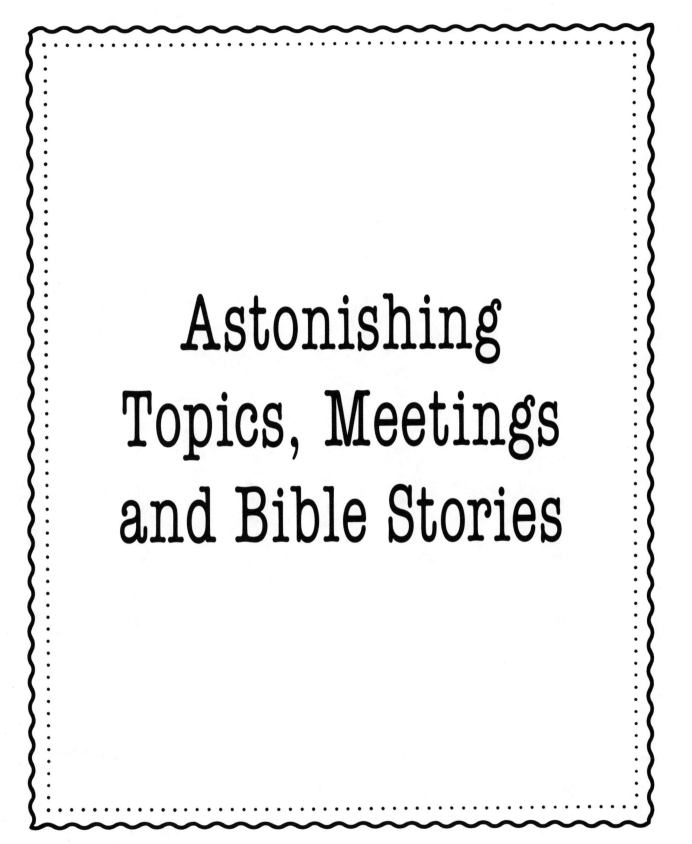

Astonishing Topics, Meetings and Bible Stories

Jonah: down in the mouth

Jonah: down in the mouth

Goliath dieth

Goliath dieth

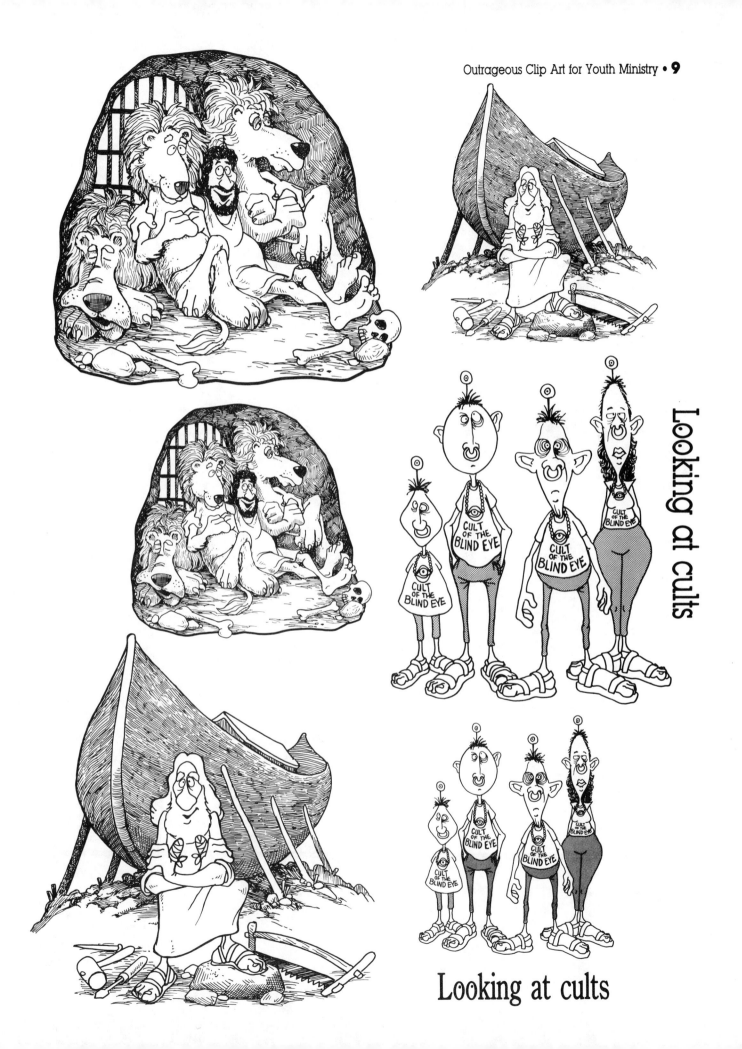

Looking at cults

in a bind?

the END

THE END IS NEAR

in a bind?

the END

THE END IS NEAR

in a bind?

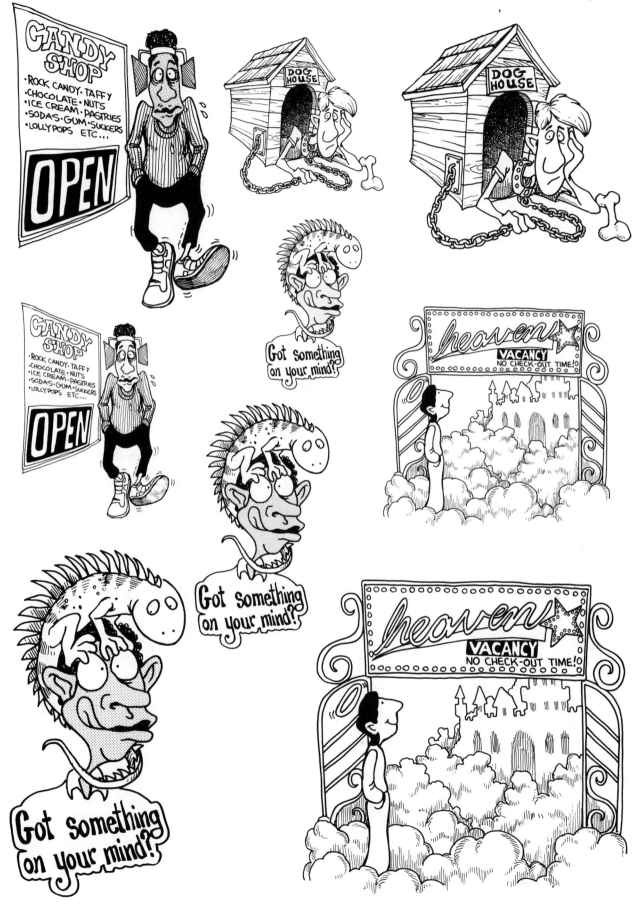

Grow for it

Spiritual growth

BibleStudy

Spiritual growth

BibleStudy

Grow for it

Church

Church

Church

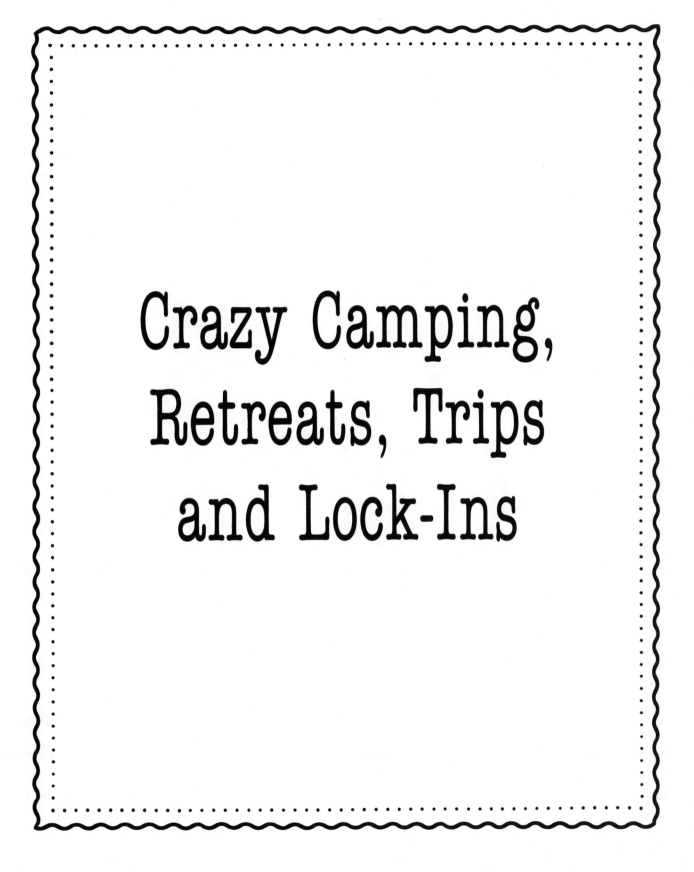

Crazy Camping, Retreats, Trips and Lock-Ins

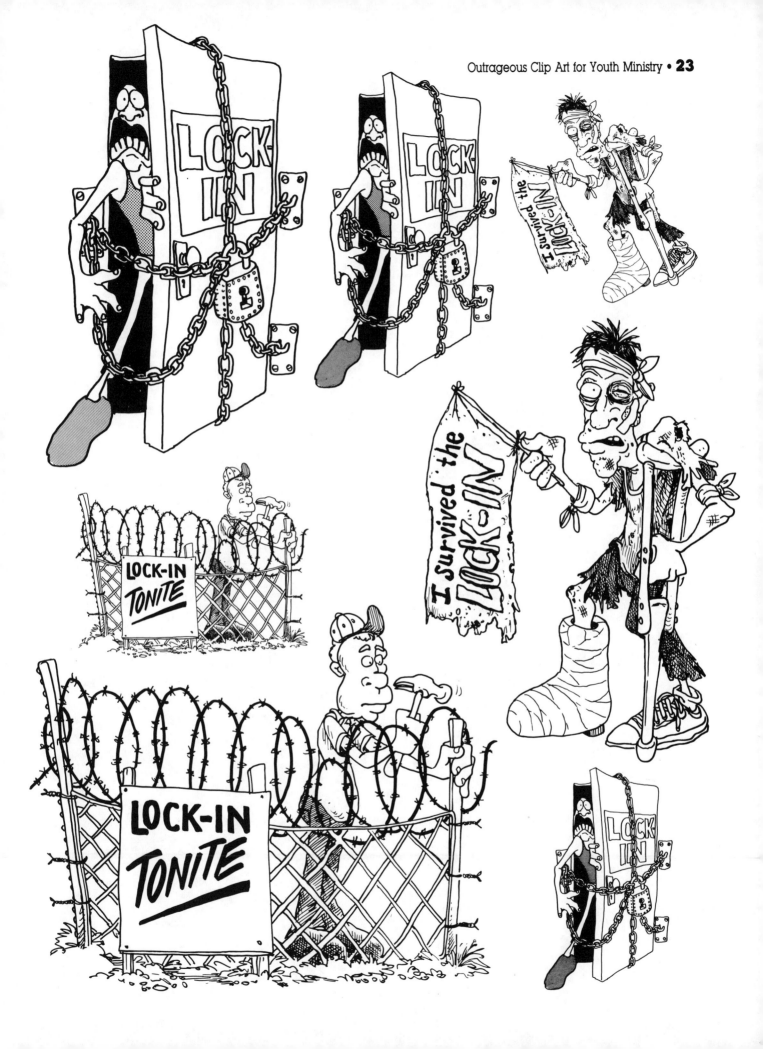

Fired up for camping

Fired up for camping

Take a hike

Who's afraid of the dark?

Hiking

Take a hike

Hiking

Who's afraid of the dark?

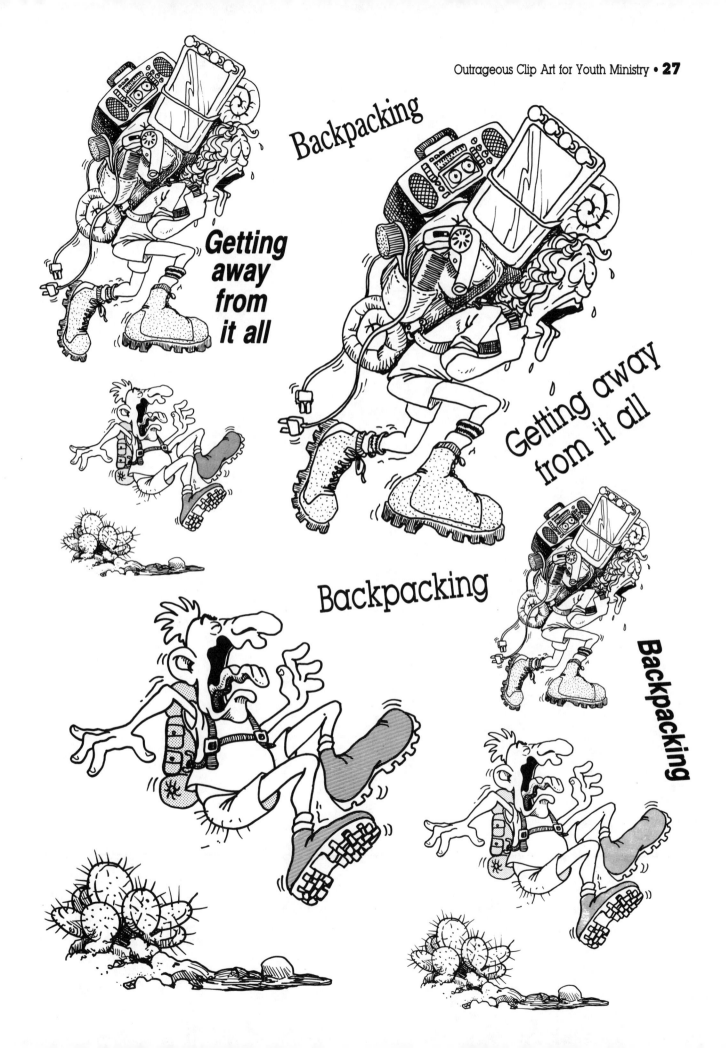

Horseback
Riding

Giddyup

Giddyup

Advance to the retreat

Giddyup

Horseback Riding

Advance
to the
retreat

Rally

Rally

Road Trip

Road Trip

Road Trip

Creatures, Characters and Other Kooks

Missing you!

Missing you!

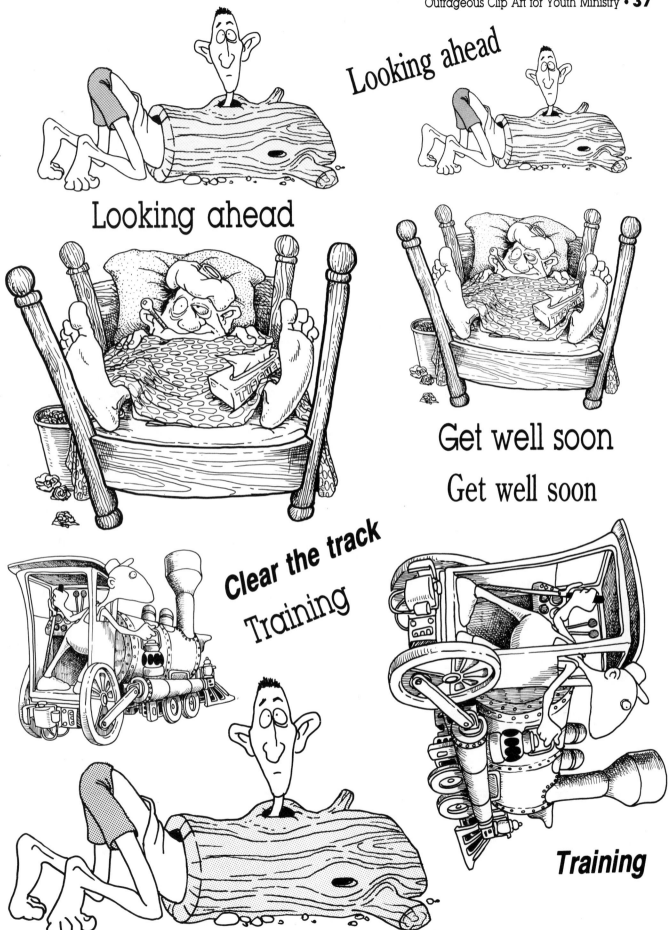

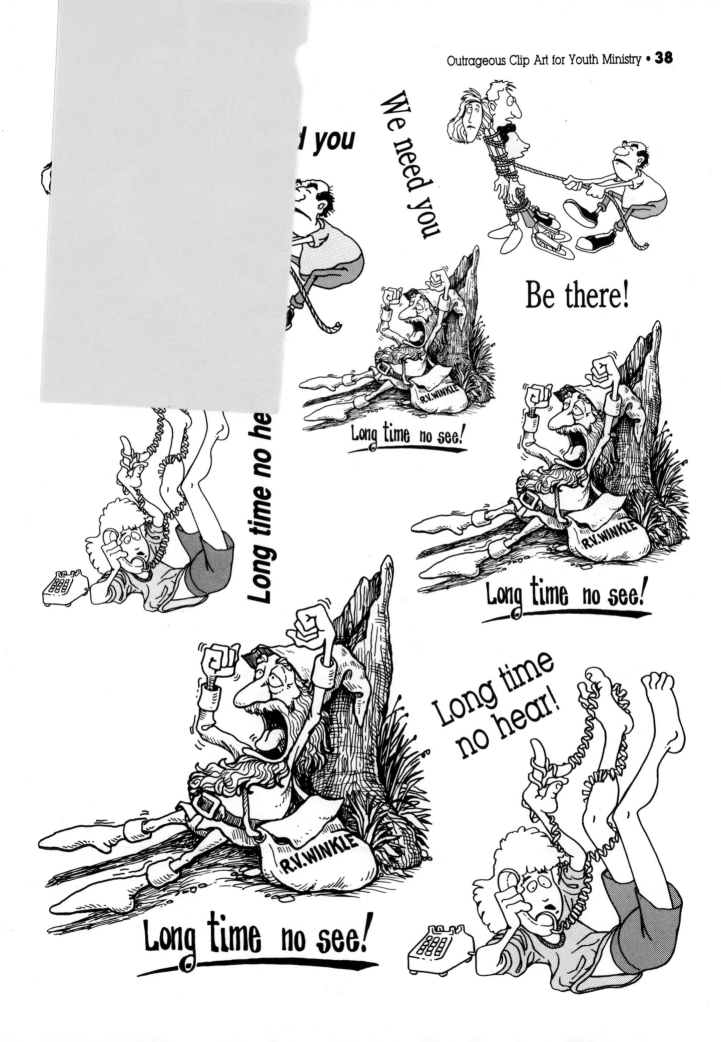

Everyone's welcome

Tea Time

Group hug

Friends

Friends

Group hug

Tea Time

Everyone's welcome

Exorbitant Entertainment, Talent Shows, Activities and Events

The picnic pack

Frisbee Fling

Frisbee Fling

Beach Party

Beach Party

The picnic pack

Show Time

Show Time

Kite Flying

Movie Night

"Cat"astrophe

Movie Night

"Reel" fun

Potpourri

Flying high

"Cat"astrophe

Kite Flying

Potpourri

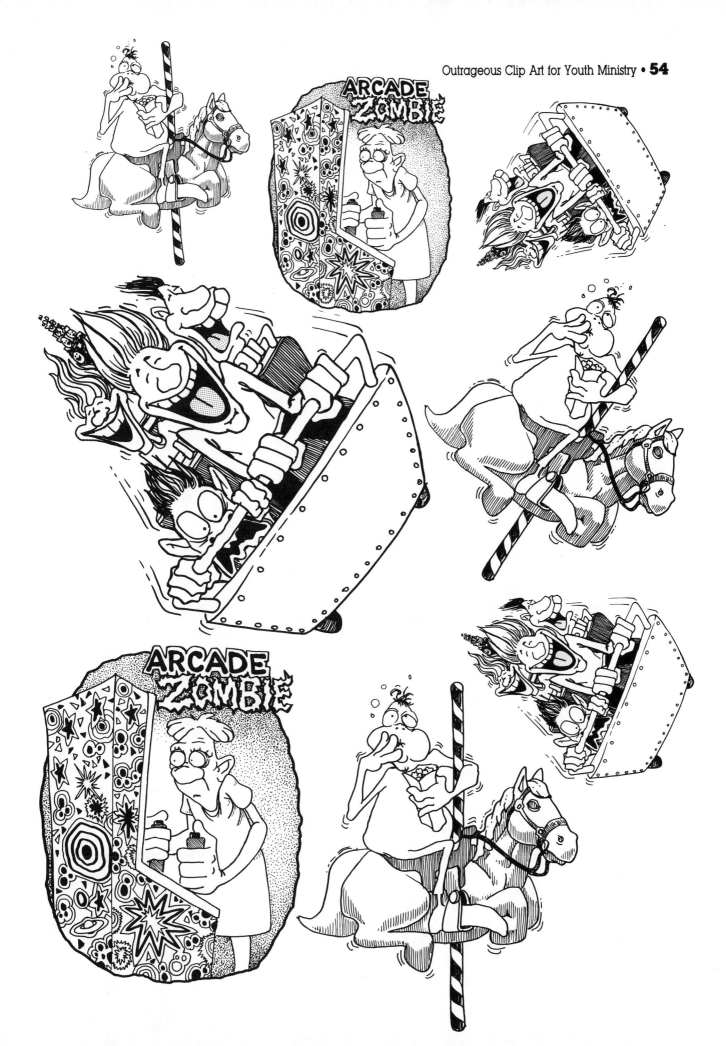

Far-Outrageous Food Frenzy

Dinner is served

Food!

Banana Split Night

B.Y.O.B.

(Bring Your Own Banana)

Food!

B.Y.O.B. (Bring Your Own Banana)

Banana Split Night

FOOD!

Dinner is served

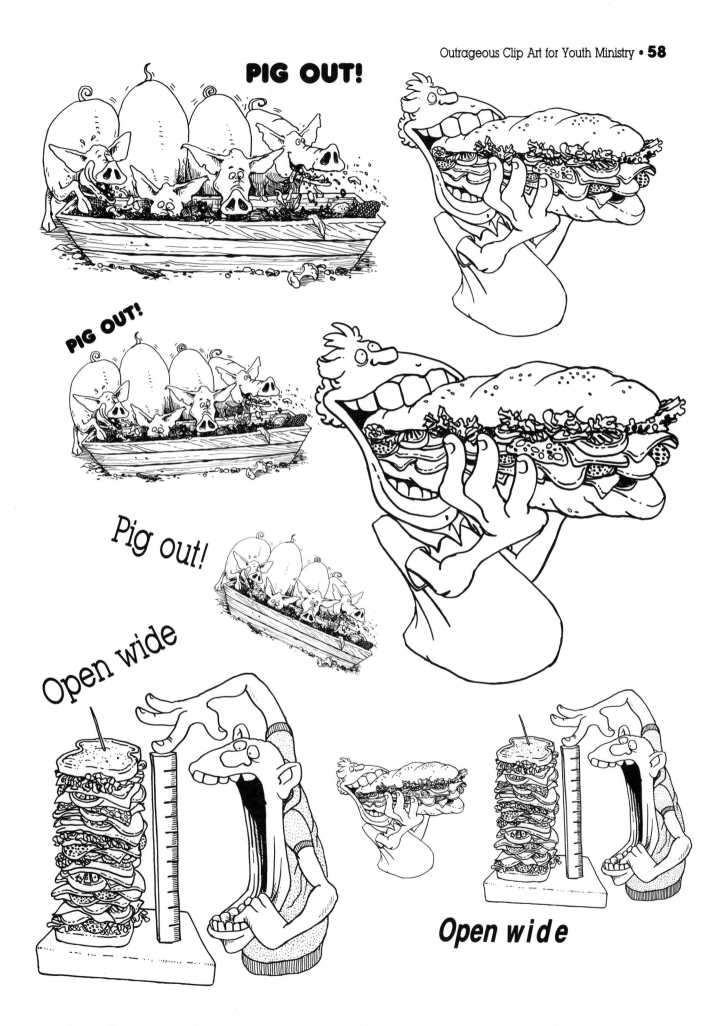

Lunch Munch

Getting to "nose" you

Progressive Dinner

Getting to "nose" you

Progressive Dinner

A balanced breakfast

A BALANCED BREAKFAST

Taco Fiesta

A dreamy dessert

Out for ice cream

Out for ice cream

Taco Fiesta

A dreamy dessert

LOW-CALORIE

LOW-CALORIE

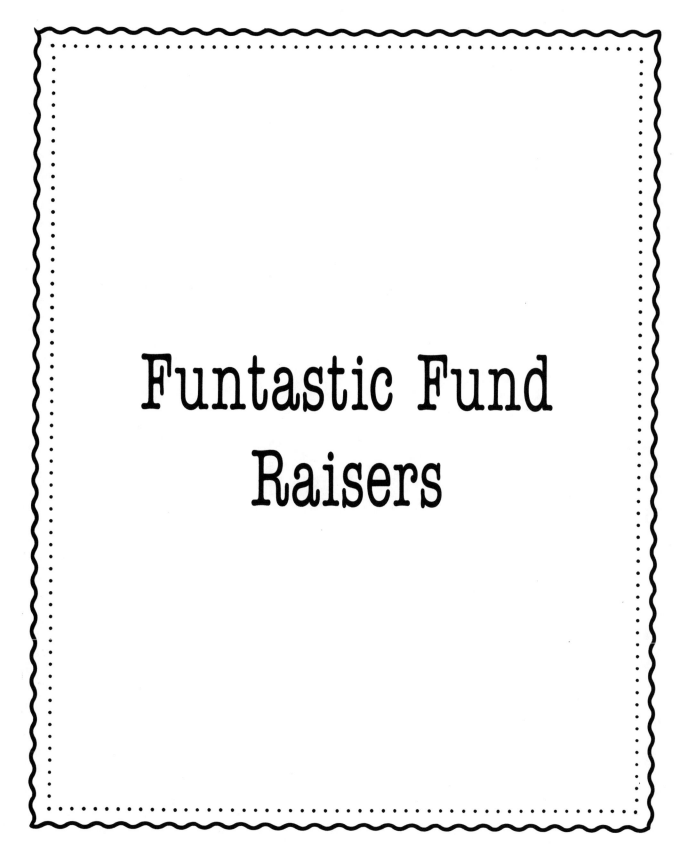

Funtastic Fund Raisers

Slave Auction

Slave Auction

Garage Sale

Garage Sale

Fund Raising

Fund Raising

Fund Rai$ing

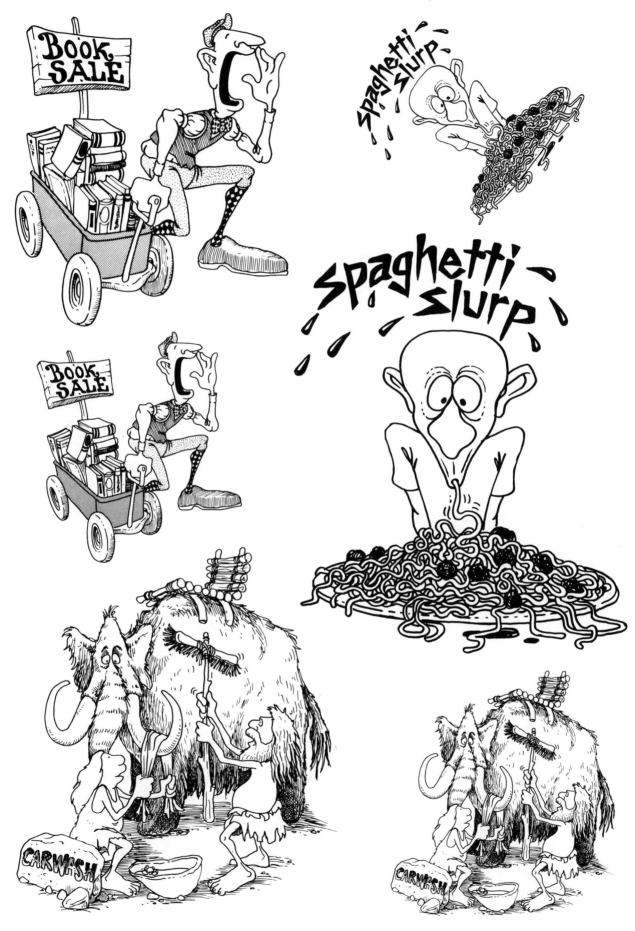

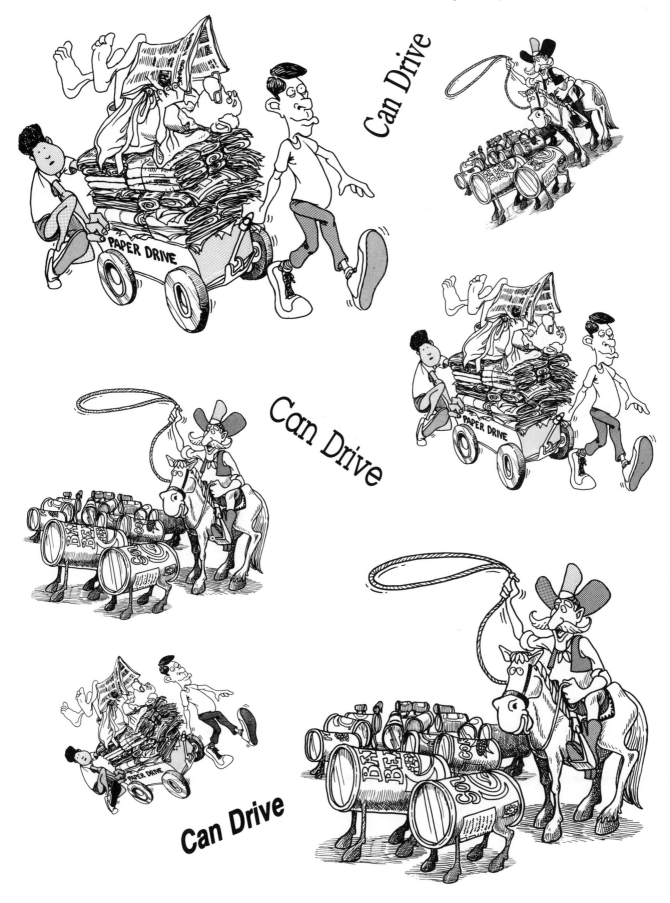

Can Drive

Can Drive

Can Drive

Hilarious Happenings and Holidays

Time flies when
you're having fun

Super Bowl
Party

Super Bowl Party

Sonrise Service

Easter

Pentecost

Pentecost

Sonrise Service

Sonrise Service

Easter

Easter

HE IS RISEN

HE IS RISEN

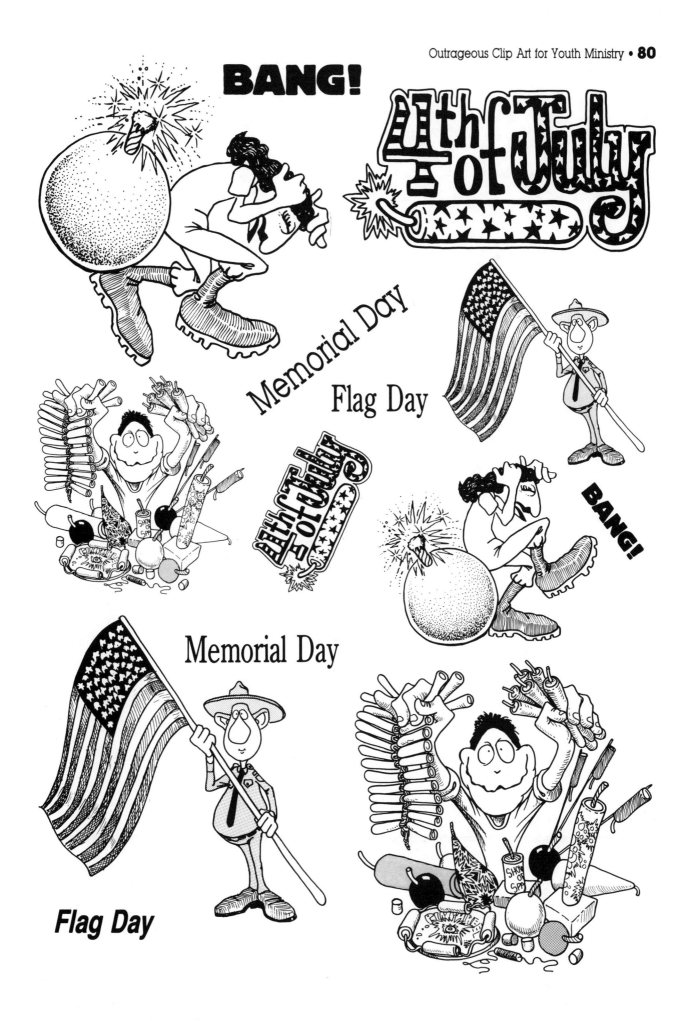

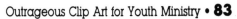

Incognito

What's for dinner?

What's for dinner?

Incognito

Incognito

Stumped?

Howling holiday carols

Howling holiday carols

Stumped?

# Christmas

Christ is born!

Noel

Noel

Noel

Christ is born!

Christ is born!

School Daze,
Home and
Work Craze

Shop Class

Shop Class

Shop Class

All in a day's work

Creativity plus!

Marching Band

Marching Band

Creativity plus!

Exams

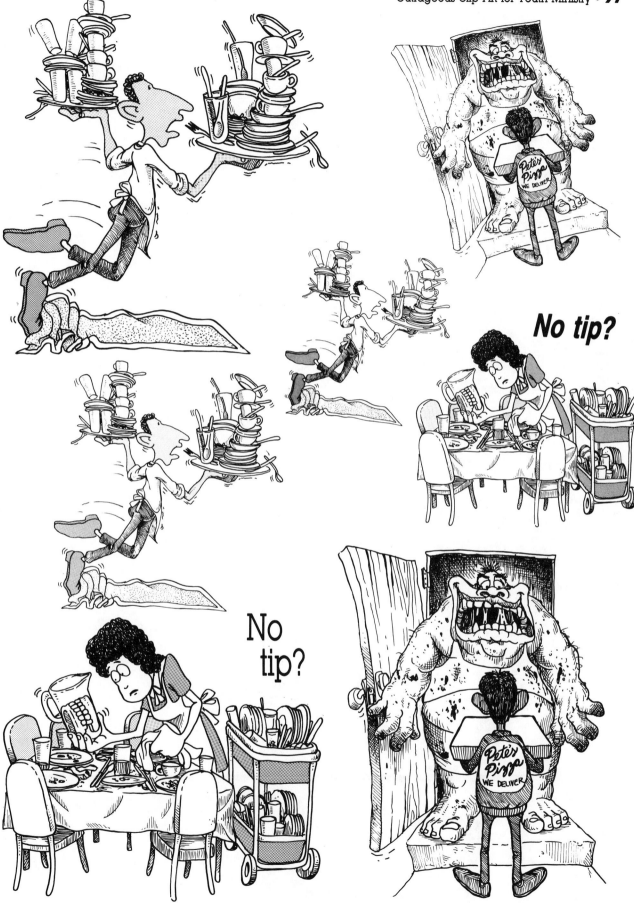

No tip?

No tip?

Try this on for size

Try this on for size

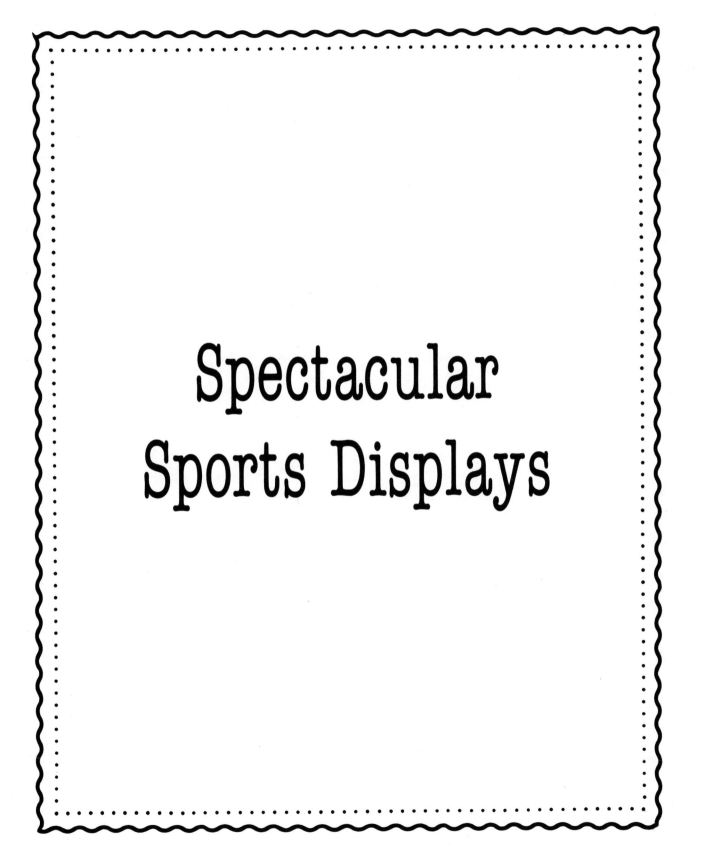

Spectacular
Sports Displays

Ice Skating

Slip sliding away

Ice Skating

Slip sliding away

Slip sliding away

Ice Skating

"The score is love-love"

"The score is love-love"

Roller Derby

Skate board

Skate board

Roller Derby

Skate board

Working the bugs out

Bike Hike

Bike Hike

Working the bugs out

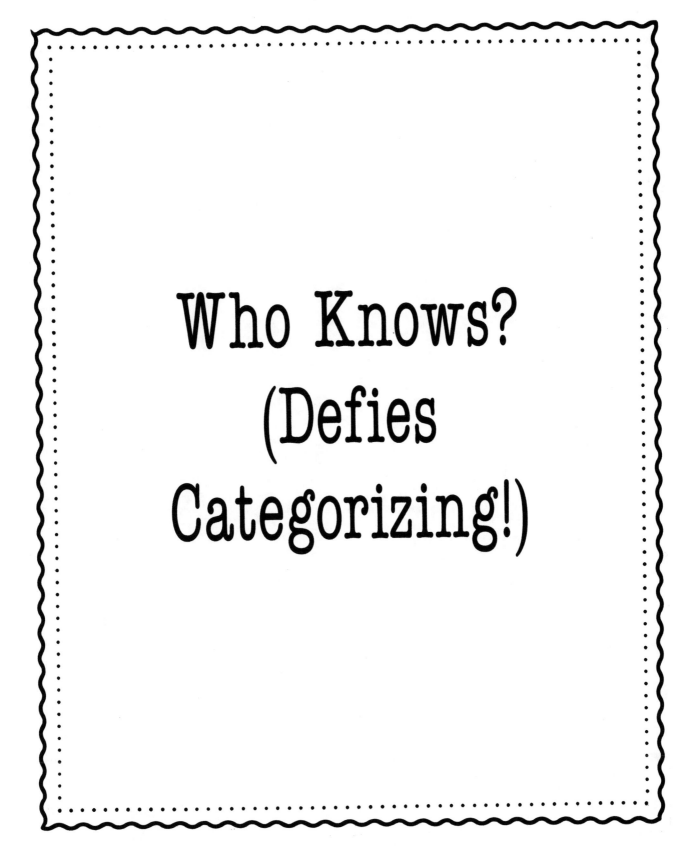

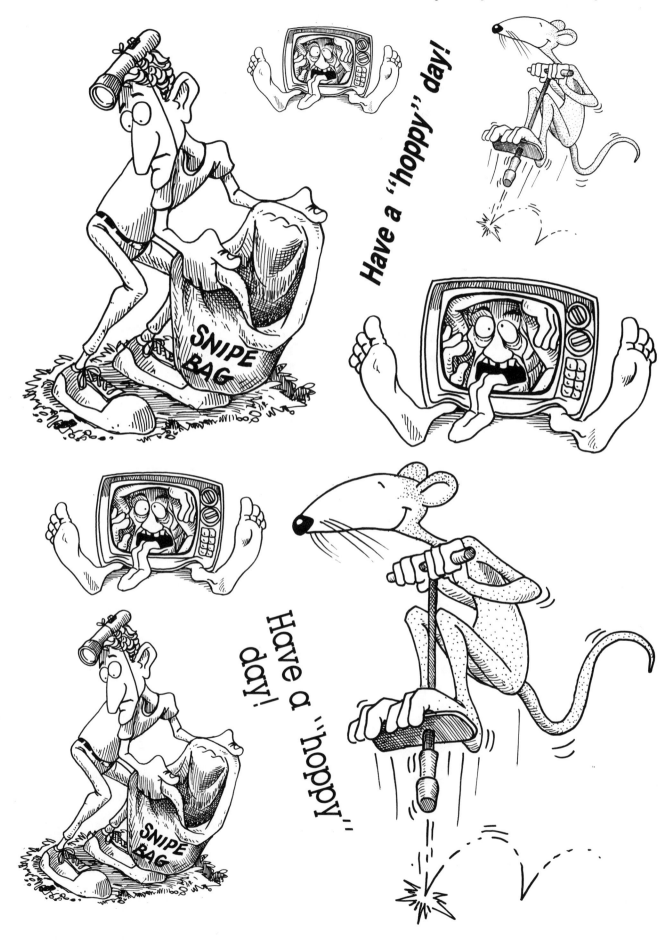

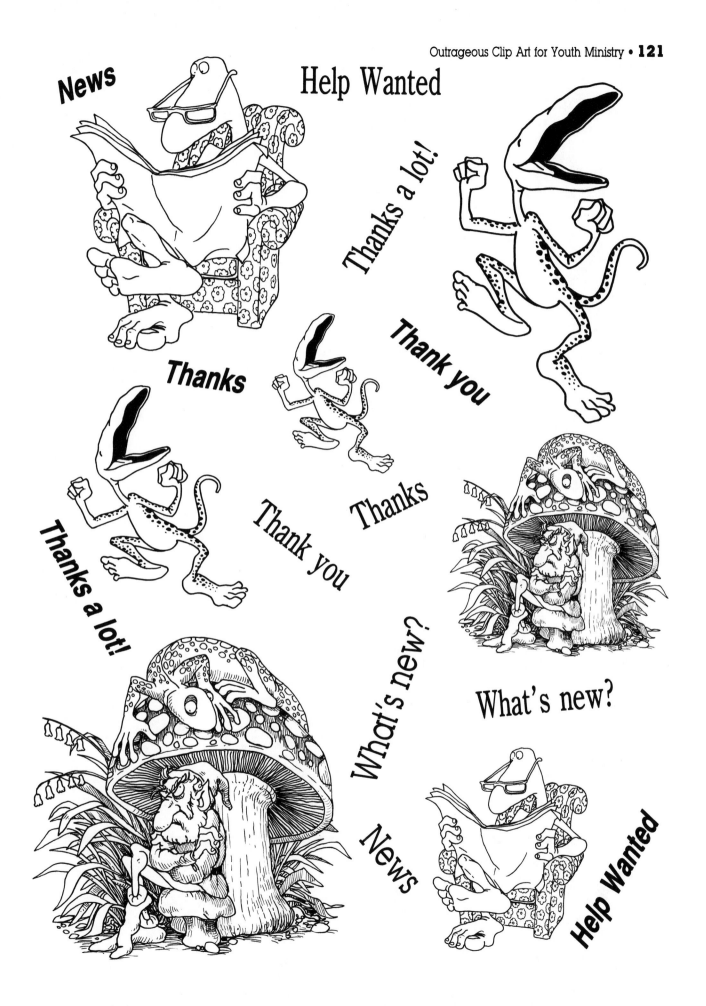

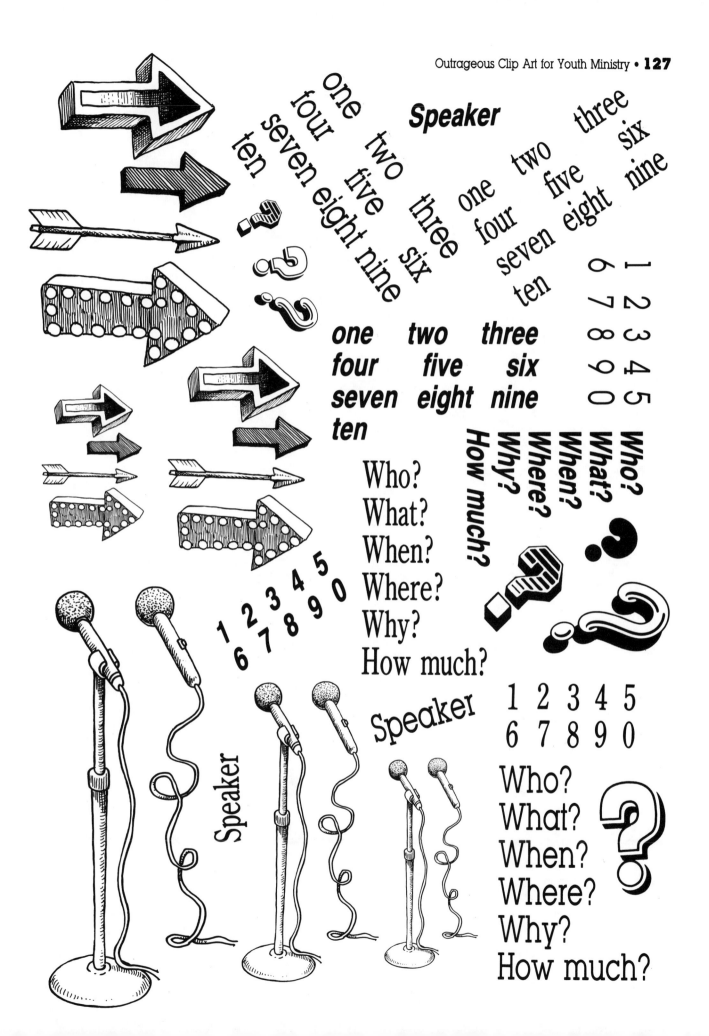

HI

Welcome Friends

Outrageous

ZAP

BOO

BOOM

hilarious

HELLO

WILD

BONK

Wonderful

ASTONISHING

Happy

WACKY

PARTY PATROL

Birthday To You

HELP!

Slurp

Spectacular

BELIEVE IT OR NOT

Happy, happy day

Ya'll come

Have a gorgeous day

That's incredible

Coming soon to a youth group near you

REGISTER

ROWDY

SURPRISE!

How 'bout that?

 Thanks

We Miss You

CRASH

SIGN UP

Goodbye

One and only

Coming soon to a youth group near you

BELIEVE IT OR NOT

BOO Happy Birthday

Ya'll come To You Spectacular

HELP! HI We Miss You

Happy, happy day HELLO

Wonderful REGISTER

 KAPOW

WELCOME FRIENDS

Announcements

Index